Abraham Lincoln

by Lucia Raatma

Compass Point Early Biographies

Content Adviser: Professor Sherry L. Field,
Department of Social Science Education, College of Education,
The University of Georgia

Reading Adviser: Dr. Linda D. Labbo,
Department of Reading Education, College of Education,
The University of Georgia

COMPASS POINT BOOKS

Minneapolis, Minnesota

Compass Point Books
3109 West 50th Street, #115
Minneapolis, MN 55410

Visit Compass Point Books on the Internet at *www.compasspointbooks.com* or e-mail your
request to *custserv@compasspointbooks.com*

Editors: E. Russell Primm and Emily J. Dolbear
Photo Researcher: Svetlana Zhurkina
Photo Selector: Dawn Friedman
Design: Bradfordesign, Inc.

Library of Congress Cataloging-in-Publication Data

Raatma, Lucia.
    Abraham Lincoln / by Lucia Raatma.
        p. cm. — (Compass Point early biographies)
    Includes bibliographical references and index.
    Summary: A brief biography of the sixteenth president, known as a wise and compassionate man
and an eloquent speaker, whose determination helped preserve the Union during the Civil War.
    ISBN 0-7565-0012-5 (hardcover)
    ISBN 0-7565-1163-1 (paperback)
        1. Lincoln, Abraham, 1809–1865—Juvenile literature. 2. Presidents—United States—
Biography—Juvenile literature. [1. Lincoln, Abraham, 1809–1865. 2. Presidents.] I. Title. II. Series.
    E457.905 .R25 2000
    973.7'092—dc21   00-008635

Table of Contents

Honest Abe

Abraham Lincoln was the sixteenth president of the United States. He was known for being kind and fair. Many people called him "Honest Abe." He was an important person in the history of the United States.

◄ Abraham Lincoln's face is one of the most famous in American history.

Early Life

Abraham Lincoln was born on February 12, 1809, in the state of Kentucky. His first home was a log cabin. The floor was made of dirt. The family's blankets were made of animal skins.

Later, Abraham and his family lived on a farm. He chopped wood and learned to build a fire. He helped his father plant crops and tend the fields.

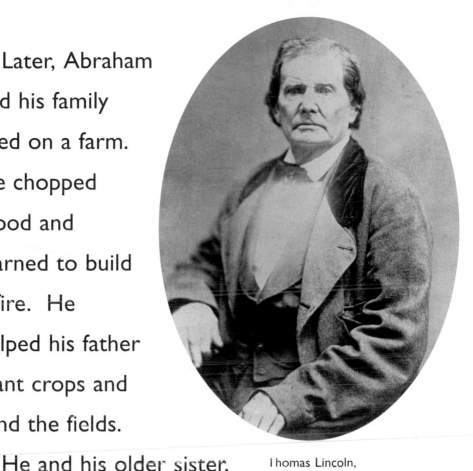

Thomas Lincoln, Abraham's father

He and his older sister, Sarah, went to school 2 miles (3 kilometers) away. They walked there each day. He learned to read, write, and do arithmetic.

◄ The birthplace of Abraham Lincoln

Sarah Bush Lincoln,
Abraham's stepmother

Abraham's mother died when he was only nine years old. Abraham's father knew that his family needed a mother. So he remarried. Abraham's stepmother took good care of Abraham and Sarah. She was very patient. She wanted Abraham to study and learn. Abraham said, "She was the best friend I ever had."

A Book Lover

Abraham worked hard on the family farm. Often there was little time for him to go to school. But Abraham loved to read. He always had a book with him. He would read between **chores**.

Abraham read all kinds of books. He even read about the law. And sometimes, he would walk into town and visit the courthouse. He enjoyed watching the lawyers at work.

Abraham earned his first dollar by rowing a boat.

On His Own

When Abraham was twenty-one, he moved to New Salem, Illinois. There he worked in a **general store**. People soon heard about Abraham Lincoln. They talked about how honest he was. Once he walked 6 miles (10 kilometers) to return a few pennies to a customer.

◀ Splitting logs was one of many chores Abraham did on the farm.

As a Soldier

In 1832, the Black Hawk War began. A group of Indians led by Chief Black Hawk fought the U.S. Army to get their land back. They were soon defeated. During this war, Abraham Lincoln became a soldier and he was trained to fight. He was in the army for only thirty days and never had to fight. But he lived with other soldiers. He saw how hard life in the army could be.

13

Abraham Lincoln as a young man

A New Job

After the Black Hawk War, Abraham ran for election to the Illinois state government, or **legislature**. He lost, but he became known throughout the state. People liked his short speeches and the way he talked to the crowd.

Later Abraham opened his own general store. But he was not a good businessman. Soon the store closed.

In May 1833, Abraham Lincoln was named **postmaster** of New Salem. He liked this job very much. It gave him time to read. And he could read every newspaper for free.

In Politics and the Law

In 1834, Abraham Lincoln ran for the Illinois legislature again. This time he won. He enjoyed **politics**, and the other lawmakers liked him. He made up his own mind and he told the truth.

Over time, Abraham Lincoln decided he wanted to be a lawyer. He studied and learned all that he could. In 1836, he became a lawyer.

Abraham Lincoln as a lawyer in court

The next year, he moved to the new state capital of Illinois—Springfield. The state capital had recently moved there from Vandalia. In Springfield, he began to work as a lawyer and enjoyed the social life.

Soon Abraham met Mary Todd. They were married in 1842.

Mary Todd Lincoln

16

Lincoln and Slavery

In the 1850s, slavery was a big problem. Slaves worked on farms and large farms called **plantations**. They had no freedom. White men owned them as if they were property.

Some states supported slavery. Other states felt it was wrong. Abraham Lincoln thought slavery was cruel and unfair. He worried that the disagreement would break the country apart.

Slaves working on a farm

In 1858, Abraham Lincoln ran for the U.S. Senate. Stephen Douglas, who supported slavery, ran against him. The two men argued about slavery at public meetings. Abraham Lincoln often won the arguments. But he lost the election.

Becoming President

Abraham Lincoln knew that the United States was in trouble. The Northern states were against slavery and the Southern states supported it. Many people in the South felt that slavery was important to their way of life. Abraham Lincoln wanted to help the country. He decided to run for the presidency.

He won! Abraham Lincoln was elected president of the United States in 1860.

◄ Stephen Douglas stands behind Abraham Lincoln while he gives a speech.

The Civil War

A year later, the Civil War began. The Southern states battled the Northern states. Thousands of Americans on both sides were killed. Abraham Lincoln hated the idea of war. He felt great

Lincoln with a general at a Civil War army camp

sorrow at the loss of so many lives. But his main goal was to save the country.

Abraham Lincoln knew that the question of slavery had to be settled. He knew that many people would disagree with his actions.

In January 1863, Abraham Lincoln signed the Emancipation Proclamation. That law freed the slaves and ended slavery.

That same year, Abraham Lincoln gave an important speech after the Battle of Gettysburg. It became one of the most famous speeches in the history of the United States.

Giving the Gettysburg Address

The End of War

In 1864, Abraham Lincoln was elected president again. But he was very tired. The Civil War had been very difficult for the country. So many Americans had died, and the country was still divided.

At last, on April 9, 1865, the South **surrendered**. The Civil War was over, and Abraham Lincoln was happy.

The South surrenders. ➤

A Sad Death

John Wilkes Booth

Five days later, on April 14, 1865, Abraham and Mary went to a play at Ford's Theatre. Suddenly a shot rang out. The president had been shot by John Wilkes Booth. Booth supported slavery and did not like what Abraham Lincoln had done.

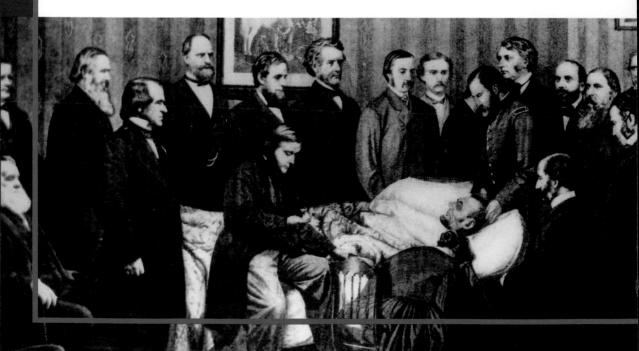

Many people honored the memory of Abraham Lincoln.

Doctors tried to help Abraham Lincoln. But he died the next morning.

Many Americans were sad when Abraham Lincoln died. Slowly, a train carrying Lincoln's body moved across the country. He was buried in Springfield, Illinois.

◄ Doctors tried to save Abraham Lincoln's life after he was shot.

An Important Life

Abraham Lincoln was a kindhearted and fair man. He worked hard to make the United States a better place. The American people valued him even more after he was gone. Today, the Lincoln Memorial in Washington, D.C., honors our sixteenth president– Abraham Lincoln.

The Lincoln Memorial

◄ This huge marble statue of Abraham Lincoln sits inside the Lincoln Memorial.

Important Dates in Abraham Lincoln's Life

1809	Born on February 12 in Kentucky
1818	His mother dies; his father remarries the next year
1832	Serves in the army during the Black Hawk War
1833	Becomes postmaster in New Salem
1834	Is elected to the Illinois General Assembly
1836	Becomes a lawyer
1842	Marries Mary Todd
1858	Runs for senate seat from Illinois; loses to Stephen Douglas
1860	Is elected sixteenth president of the United States
1861–1865	The Civil War takes place
1863	Signs the Emancipation Proclamation; delivers the Gettysburg Address
1864	Is elected president again
1865	Shot on April 14 at Ford's Theatre; dies on April 15

Glossary

chores—jobs around the house or the farm

general store—a place that sells food and many other things

legislature—a part of government

plantations—large farms

politics—government

postmaster—person in charge of a post office

surrendered—gave up

Did You Know?

- Abraham Lincoln carried bills and legal papers in his tall stovepipe hat.

- At 6 feet, 4 inches (190 centimeters), Abraham Lincoln was the tallest U.S. president.

- Abraham Lincoln was the first U.S. president to be killed in office.

Want to Know More?

At the Library

Borden, Louise A. *Lincoln and Me*. New York: Scholastic, 1999.

Schaefer, Lola. *Abraham Lincoln*. Mankato, Minn.: Capstone Press, 1998.

Shorto, Russell. *Abraham Lincoln and the End of Slavery*. Gateway. Brookfield, Conn.: Millbrook Press, 1994.

On the Web

For more information on *Abraham Lincoln,* use FactHound
to track down Web sites related to this book.

1. Go to *www.facthound.com*
2. Type in a search word related to this book
   or this book ID: 0756500125
3. Click on the *Fetch It* button.

Your trusty FactHound will fetch the best Web sites for you!

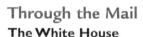

Through the Mail

The White House

1600 Pennsylvania Avenue, N.W.

Washington, DC 20500-0001

For information about the presidency

On the Road

The Lincoln Memorial

National Capital Parks-Central

The National Mall

900 Ohio Drive, S.W.

Washington, DC 20242

202/426-6841

To visit the national monument

Index

About the Author

Lucia Raatma received her bachelor's degree in English literature from the University of South Carolina and her master's degree in cinema studies from New York University. She has written a wide range of books for young people. When she is not researching or writing, she enjoys going to movies, playing tennis, and spending time with her husband, daughter, and golden retriever.